The Path: Breaking the Chains of Resentment, The Power of Forgiveness in the Church

Sharon Cooper-Jones

Published by Sharon Cooper-Jones, 2024.

While every precaution has been taken in the preparation of this book, the publisher assumes no responsibility for errors or omissions, or for damages resulting from the use of the information contained herein.

THE PATH: BREAKING THE CHAINS OF RESENTMENT, THE POWER OF FORGIVENESS IN THE CHURCH

First edition. January 15, 2024.

ISBN: 979-8224120642

Written by Sharon Cooper-Jones.

Table of Contents

Chapter 1: The Power of Forgiveness

Understanding Resentment in the Church

Resentment is a powerful emotion that can wreak havoc within the walls of a church. It can create divisions, hinder spiritual growth, and undermine the transformative power of forgiveness. In this subchapter, we will delve into the depths of resentment and its detrimental effects within the church community. By understanding the root causes and consequences of resentment, we can begin to break free from its chains and embrace the true power of forgiveness.

Resentment often arises from unmet expectations, perceived injustices, or unresolved conflicts. It can stem from disagreements over leadership, differences in theological interpretations, or even personal grievances between members. When left unaddressed, these resentful feelings can fester and poison the environment of love, compassion, and unity that should characterize any church community.

One of the consequences of resentment within the church is the erosion of trust and unity. Resentment can lead to gossip, backbiting, and a breakdown in communication, creating an atmosphere of suspicion and discord. This hinders the church's ability to fulfill its mission and live out the transformative power of forgiveness. It becomes difficult to extend grace and love to others when resentment takes hold.

Another consequence is the hindrance of spiritual growth. Resentment blinds us to our own faults and weaknesses, preventing us from humbly seeking forgiveness and reconciliation. It stifles our ability to extend forgiveness to others, inhibiting our own spiritual journey. By understanding the destructive nature of resentment, we can actively work towards dismantling its hold on our hearts and minds, allowing for personal and communal growth.

However, breaking free from the chains of resentment is not an easy task. It requires a commitment to self-reflection, humility, and a willingness to forgive. The transformative power of forgiveness can heal wounds, restore relationships, and foster a sense of unity within the church. By extending grace to one another, we create an environment that embraces growth, understanding, and acceptance.

In conclusion, understanding resentment in the church is crucial in order to experience the transformative power of forgiveness. By recognizing the root causes and consequences of resentment, we can actively work towards breaking free from its grip. Let us strive to create a church community that fosters forgiveness, unity, and love, allowing the transformative power of forgiveness to work within us and through us. Only then can we truly break the chains of resentment and experience the abundant life that Christ has called us to.

Recognizing the signs of resentment

Resentment is a common emotion that lurks beneath the surface of many individuals, including those within the church community. It can slowly poison relationships, hinder personal growth, and hinder the transformative power of forgiveness. In this subchapter, we will explore the signs of resentment and how to recognize them in ourselves and others.

One of the key signs of resentment is a persistent feeling of anger or bitterness towards someone or something. It may manifest as a deep-seated grudge that refuses to fade away, even after time has passed. Often, individuals experiencing resentment will find themselves replaying past events or conversations in their minds, fueling their negative emotions further.

Another telltale sign of resentment is a lack of empathy or understanding towards the person or situation that has caused the resentment. Rather than seeking to understand the other person's perspective, those who harbor resentment tend to hold onto their own feelings of hurt or betrayal, creating a barrier to reconciliation and forgiveness.

Resentment can also manifest physically, affecting our overall well-being. Headaches, stomachaches, and tension in the body are common physical symptoms of resentment. Additionally, it may lead to sleep disturbances, increased stress levels, and a general sense of dissatisfaction with life.

Recognizing these signs within ourselves is the first step towards breaking the chains of resentment. It requires self-reflection, honesty, and a willingness to confront and address our own emotions. By acknowledging our resentment, we open the door to healing and transformation.

However, as church members, it is equally essential to recognize the signs of resentment in others. This allows us to extend compassion and support to those who may be silently suffering. It provides an opportunity to reach out, offer a listening ear, and guide them towards the power of forgiveness.

By exploring the transformative power of forgiveness within the church community, we can create an environment where resentment is recognized and addressed openly. Through education, open discussions, and support groups, we can help individuals break free from the chains that hold them back and embrace the healing power of forgiveness.

In conclusion, recognizing the signs of resentment is crucial for personal growth and cultivating a community of forgiveness within the church. By understanding these signs, both in ourselves and others, we can pave the way towards a more compassionate, empathetic, and forgiving congregation. Let us embark on this journey together, breaking the chains of resentment and embracing the transformative power of forgiveness.

The detrimental effects of holding onto resentment

Resentment is a powerful emotion that can consume our hearts and minds, leading to a multitude of negative consequences. As church members, it is essential for us to understand the detrimental effects of holding onto resentment and the transformative power of forgiveness.

One of the most significant consequences of harboring resentment is the erosion of relationships. When we hold onto grudges and refuse to forgive, it creates a barrier between ourselves and others. Resentment breeds anger, bitterness, and ultimately, distance. It hinders our ability to connect with others in a meaningful and authentic way, preventing us from experiencing the love and unity that the church should foster.

Moreover, holding onto resentment takes a toll on our mental and emotional well-being. It keeps us trapped in a cycle of negativity, constantly replaying past hurts and grievances in our minds. This constant dwelling on negative experiences leads to increased stress, anxiety, and even depression. Over time, it can negatively impact our physical health as well, manifesting as sleep disturbances, weakened immune systems, and other stress-related ailments.

Furthermore, resentment hinders our spiritual growth and stifles our connection with God. The Bible teaches us the importance of forgiveness and letting go of grudges. By holding onto resentment, we are essentially closing our hearts to God's love and grace. It prevents us from experiencing the transformative power of forgiveness and the freedom that comes with it.

On the contrary, embracing forgiveness can have a profound impact on our lives as church members. Forgiveness allows us to release the burden of resentment, freeing ourselves from the chains of bitterness and anger. It opens the door for healing, restoration, and reconciliation. By choosing to forgive, we create space for God's love and grace to flow through us, enabling us to cultivate healthy relationships, both within the church and beyond.

Exploring the transformative power of forgiveness is not an easy journey. It requires vulnerability, humility, and a willingness to let go of our pride. However, the rewards far outweigh the challenges. By actively choosing forgiveness, we can experience true freedom, genuine joy, and a renewed sense of purpose within the church community.

In conclusion, holding onto resentment has detrimental effects that hinder our relationships, mental and emotional well-being, and spiritual growth. As church members, it is vital for us to recognize the destructive nature of resentment and embrace the transformative power of forgiveness. By doing so, we can break the chains of resentment and create a community that radiates love, unity, and grace.

The Biblical Call to Forgiveness

In the journey of faith, forgiveness plays a crucial role in the transformation of individuals and communities. It is a powerful force that breaks the chains of resentment and opens the door to healing and restoration. The Bible, as the ultimate source of wisdom and guidance, calls upon believers to embrace the transformative power of forgiveness in their lives.

The concept of forgiveness is woven throughout the Scriptures, from the Old Testament to the New Testament. In the Old Testament, we learn about the forgiveness of God towards His people, despite their repeated disobedience and shortcomings. The Psalms beautifully express the longing for forgiveness and the joy that comes with it. As church members, we are called to imitate God's example and extend forgiveness to others, just as He has forgiven us.

In the New Testament, the message of forgiveness reaches its pinnacle with the life and teachings of Jesus Christ. His sacrificial death on the cross was the ultimate act of forgiveness, demonstrating God's unconditional love and mercy towards humanity. Jesus taught us to pray, "Forgive us our trespasses, as we forgive those who trespass against us." These words remind us of our responsibility to forgive others, as we have been forgiven.

Forgiveness is not an easy task. It requires humility, vulnerability, and a willingness to let go of the pain and resentment that can consume our hearts. However, the rewards of forgiveness are immeasurable. It frees us from the burden of bitterness, restores broken relationships, and allows us to experience true peace and joy.

In the church, forgiveness plays a vital role in maintaining unity and fostering a culture of love and acceptance. As church members, we are called to be ambassadors of forgiveness, extending grace and mercy to one another. We must strive to create a safe and nurturing environment where healing and reconciliation can take place.

Exploring the transformative power of forgiveness is an invitation to delve deeper into God's Word and discover the richness of His love and mercy. It is a reminder that forgiveness is not just a personal act, but a radical lifestyle that has the power to impact individuals, families, and communities.

In the book "Breaking the Chains of Resentment: The Power of Forgiveness in the Church," we will explore the biblical foundations of forgiveness and its practical application in our daily lives. Through personal stories, biblical insights, and practical exercises, we will embark on a journey towards freedom and healing.

Let us embrace the biblical call to forgiveness and allow it to transform our lives and the life of our church. May we become agents of forgiveness, breaking the chains of resentment and experiencing the abundant life that Christ offers us.

Examining forgiveness in the teachings of Jesus

In the realm of exploring the transformative power of forgiveness, it is impossible to ignore the profound teachings of Jesus Christ. In his time on earth, Jesus exemplified and preached a message of forgiveness that continues to resonate with believers even today. By examining the teachings of Jesus, we can uncover the depth and significance of forgiveness in our lives and within the Church.

Jesus consistently emphasized the importance of forgiveness in his teachings, urging his followers to extend mercy and grace to others. One of the most powerful examples is found in the Lord's Prayer, where Jesus instructs his disciples to pray, "Forgive us our debts, as we also have forgiven our debtors." (Matthew 6:12) This statement underscores the reciprocal nature of forgiveness, highlighting that our own forgiveness is intricately tied to our willingness to forgive others.

Furthermore, Jesus emphasized the need for forgiveness as a means of healing and restoration. In the parable of the Prodigal Son, Jesus illustrates the compassionate nature of God, who welcomes back the wayward son with open arms, forgiving his past transgressions. Through this parable, Jesus teaches us that forgiveness holds the power to redeem and restore relationships, fostering healing and reconciliation.

Jesus also challenged his followers to extend forgiveness to their enemies. In the Sermon on the Mount, he proclaimed, "Love your enemies and pray for those who persecute you." (Matthew 5:44) This radical teaching calls us to transcend our natural inclination to hold grudges or seek revenge, instead opting for forgiveness and love. By doing so, we break the chains of resentment and open the door to transformative change within ourselves and within the Church.

The teachings of Jesus on forgiveness are not mere platitudes; they are a call to action. As church members, we are called to embody the transformative power of forgiveness in our daily lives. This means actively seeking reconciliation, extending grace, and pursuing healing in our relationships. By embracing forgiveness as a central tenet of our faith, we can break free from the bondage of resentment and experience the true power of God's love working through us.

In conclusion, examining forgiveness in the teachings of Jesus reveals its immense significance within the Church. Jesus' teachings emphasize the reciprocal nature of forgiveness, its power to heal and restore, and the need to extend forgiveness even to our enemies. As church members exploring the transformative power of forgiveness, we are called to live out these teachings in our own lives, cultivating a culture of forgiveness and grace within our church community. Through forgiveness, we can break the chains of resentment and experience the true transformative power of God's love.

Scriptural passages emphasizing the importance of forgiveness

In our quest to explore the transformative power of forgiveness, we turn to the scriptures to understand the importance of this practice in our lives as church members. The Bible is replete with passages that highlight forgiveness as a central theme, revealing its significance in our spiritual growth and relationships.

One of the most well-known scriptural passages on forgiveness is found in Matthew 6:14-15, where Jesus teaches his disciples about the power of forgiving others. He says, "For if you forgive others their trespasses, your heavenly Father will also forgive you. But if you do not forgive others, neither will your Father forgive your trespasses." This verse reminds us that forgiveness is not just a moral obligation but also a spiritual necessity. By extending forgiveness to others, we open ourselves to receiving God's forgiveness and experiencing true freedom from resentment and bitterness.

Another powerful passage that emphasizes forgiveness is found in Colossians 3:13, where the apostle Paul instructs the church members to "Bear with each other and forgive one another if any of you has a grievance against someone. Forgive as the Lord forgave you." Here, forgiveness is presented as an act of obedience to God's command, reflecting the forgiveness we have received through Christ. By forgiving others, we imitate God's love and mercy, creating an atmosphere of reconciliation and unity within the church community.

In Luke 17:3-4, Jesus teaches his disciples about the importance of forgiveness in the context of personal relationships. He says, "If your brother or sister sins against you, rebuke them; and if they repent, forgive them. Even if they sin against you seven times in a day and seven times come back to you saying, 'I repent,' you must forgive them." This passage challenges us to extend forgiveness even when it seems difficult or repetitive. It reminds us that forgiveness is not contingent upon the magnitude of the offense but rather on our willingness to let go of resentment and extend grace.

These scriptural passages, among many others, underscore the importance of forgiveness in our lives as church members. They remind us that forgiveness is not a mere act of kindness but a transformative practice that brings healing, restoration, and unity within the Body of Christ. As we embark on the journey of breaking the chains of resentment, let us immerse ourselves in the wisdom of these scriptures and embrace the power of forgiveness, both for ourselves and for others.

Breaking the Chains of Resentment

In a world filled with hurt and pain, forgiveness stands as a transformative force that has the power to heal broken hearts and mend broken relationships. As church members, we are called to explore the transformative power of forgiveness and discover how it can break the chains of resentment that hold us captive.

Resentment is a powerful emotion that can consume our thoughts and poison our souls. It builds walls between ourselves and others, preventing us from experiencing the fullness of God's love and grace. But through forgiveness, we can dismantle these barriers and find true freedom.

Forgiveness is not easy, especially when we have been deeply wounded. It requires us to let go of our desire for revenge and instead choose mercy and compassion. It is a journey that takes time and effort, but the rewards are immeasurable.

When we choose to forgive, we release ourselves from the burden of carrying the weight of resentment. We surrender our pain to a higher power, allowing God's healing love to flow through us. We are reminded of Christ's ultimate act of forgiveness on the cross, and we are empowered to follow in His footsteps.

Forgiveness does not mean forgetting or condoning the wrongs done to us. It means acknowledging the hurt and choosing to let go of the bitterness that accompanies it. It means setting ourselves free from the chains that resentment creates, enabling us to move forward with a renewed spirit.

In the church, forgiveness is not just a personal journey but a collective one. As we learn to forgive one another, we create a community built on love, grace, and understanding. We become a beacon of hope for those who are burdened by resentment, offering them a pathway to freedom and healing.

Let us embark on this journey together, breaking the chains of resentment that hold us back from experiencing the fullness of God's love. Through forgiveness, we can create a church that reflects the transformative power of grace and offers a sanctuary for all who seek solace and healing.

In the chapters ahead, we will explore the stories of individuals who have experienced the power of forgiveness firsthand. We will learn from their journeys and gain insights into how to navigate our own paths toward forgiveness. Together, we can break the chains of resentment and embrace the transformative power of forgiveness in our lives and within the church.

Acknowledging the need for personal healing

In our journey through life, we often encounter situations and experiences that leave us wounded, scarred, and burdened with resentment. These emotional wounds can weigh heavily on our hearts and souls, affecting our relationships, our spirituality, and our overall well-being. As church members, it is important for us to acknowledge the need for personal healing and embrace the transformative power of forgiveness.

Resentment is a powerful emotion that can consume us if left unattended. Holding onto grudges and refusing to forgive can create a barrier between ourselves and God, hindering our spiritual growth. It is crucial for us to recognize that forgiveness is not simply an act bestowed upon others; it is also an act of self-liberation. By forgiving, we release ourselves from the burden of anger, bitterness, and pain.

Acknowledging the need for personal healing requires us to be honest with ourselves and confront the wounds that we carry. It is an opportunity for introspection, reflection, and self-discovery. By exploring the depths of our emotions and facing the pain head-on, we can begin the process of healing and transformation.

In the church community, we often emphasize the importance of forgiveness towards others. However, we must not overlook the significance of self-forgiveness. It is essential for us to extend the same compassion, understanding, and grace to ourselves as we do to others. Recognizing our own faults, mistakes, and shortcomings is not an act of self-condemnation but a step towards personal growth and healing.

Acknowledging the need for personal healing also requires us to seek support from our church community. We are not meant to walk this journey alone. By opening up to trusted individuals within our congregation, we create a safe space where healing can take place. Sharing our struggles, doubts, and pain with others allows us to receive comfort, encouragement, and guidance.

As we embark on the process of personal healing, we must remember that forgiveness is not a one-time event but a lifelong practice. It is a continuous choice that we make every day. By acknowledging our need for personal healing, exploring the transformative power of forgiveness, and seeking support from our church community, we can break the chains of resentment and experience the liberating power of forgiveness in our lives. Let us embrace this journey of healing with open hearts and minds, knowing that through forgiveness, we can find true freedom and restoration.

Finding strength in forgiveness

In the journey of life, we all face moments of hurt, betrayal, and disappointment. These experiences can leave us burdened with resentment, anger, and a desire for revenge. However, as members of the church, we are called to a higher purpose – to explore the transformative power of forgiveness.

In this subchapter, titled "Finding Strength in Forgiveness," we delve into the incredible strength that forgiveness brings into our lives. Forgiveness is not a sign of weakness; rather, it is a demonstration of inner strength and courage. It is a conscious decision to release the shackles of resentment and choose love and compassion instead.

When we hold on to grudges and refuse to forgive, we allow negativity to consume our hearts and minds. It becomes a heavy burden that hinders our spiritual growth and prevents us from experiencing true joy and peace. However, when we embrace forgiveness, we unleash a powerful force that can heal wounds, restore relationships, and even transform our own lives.

Forgiveness provides us with the opportunity to break free from the chains of resentment and bitterness. It empowers us to let go of the past and embrace a future filled with hope, love, and understanding. By forgiving those who have wronged us, we set ourselves free from the burden of carrying their actions with us.

Furthermore, forgiveness allows us to cultivate empathy and compassion. As we extend forgiveness to others, we begin to see them through the lens of humanity – flawed yet deserving of love and understanding. It helps us move beyond judgment and condemnation, creating a space for healing and reconciliation.

In the church, forgiveness plays a vital role in fostering unity and harmony among its members. When we forgive one another, we create an environment of love and acceptance, where healing and growth can flourish. It is through forgiveness that we can truly live out the teachings of Christ and embody His grace and mercy.

In conclusion, finding strength in forgiveness is not only a personal journey but also a transformative experience that impacts our relationships, our church, and our spiritual growth. It requires courage, humility, and a deep understanding of the power of forgiveness. As we explore this transformative power, may we embrace forgiveness as a way of life, breaking the chains of resentment and experiencing the true freedom and strength that forgiveness brings.

Chapter 2: Overcoming Barriers to Forgiveness

The Role of Pride in Hindering Forgiveness

In our journey towards exploring the transformative power of forgiveness, it is essential to delve into the role of pride in hindering this process. As church members, we are called to embrace forgiveness wholeheartedly, yet pride often erects barriers that prevent us from experiencing the true freedom and healing that forgiveness brings.

Pride manifests itself in various ways, often disguising itself as self-righteousness or a sense of superiority. It convinces us that we are justified in holding onto resentment, that we are somehow above the need to forgive. This distorted perception not only damages our relationships with others but also hinders our spiritual growth.

One of the primary ways pride hampers forgiveness is by feeding our ego and fostering a sense of entitlement. We may believe that we have been wronged, and therefore, we deserve to hold onto our anger and resentment. This attitude prevents us from extending grace and understanding to those who have hurt us, perpetuating a cycle of bitterness and brokenness.

Furthermore, pride often leads to a lack of empathy and compassion. When we are consumed by our own pride, we are unable to see beyond our own hurt and pain. We become blind to the struggles and weaknesses of others, making it nearly impossible to extend forgiveness. Our pride convinces us that forgiveness is a sign of weakness, rather than the transformative act of strength that it truly is.

Additionally, pride can prevent us from acknowledging our own faults and seeking forgiveness from others. We may find it challenging to admit our mistakes and ask for forgiveness, fearing that it will diminish our reputation or make us appear vulnerable. This refusal to humbly seek forgiveness not only damages our relationships but also hinders our own spiritual growth and prevents us from experiencing the fullness of God's grace.

To break the chains of resentment, we must humbly confront our pride and recognize its destructive influence on our ability to forgive. By acknowledging our own vulnerabilities and surrendering our pride to God, we open ourselves up to the transformative power of forgiveness. Let us strive to cultivate a spirit of humility, embracing the understanding that forgiveness is not a sign of weakness but a testament to the strength of our faith.

In conclusion, pride plays a significant role in hindering forgiveness within the church community. By recognizing the destructive influence of pride and humbly surrendering it to God, we can break free from the chains of resentment and experience the transformative power of forgiveness. Let us strive to cultivate a spirit of humility and extend grace and understanding to others, fostering healing and reconciliation within our church family.

Understanding the dangers of pride in the church

In the journey of exploring the transformative power of forgiveness, it is crucial to address the issue of pride. Pride, although often overlooked, can have devastating consequences within the church community. It is essential for church members to recognize and understand the dangers that pride poses to the unity and spiritual growth of the church.

First and foremost, pride creates division among believers. When pride takes root in the hearts of individuals, it fosters a sense of superiority and self-righteousness. This leads to judgment and a critical spirit, ultimately creating a rift within the church. Instead of fostering love, understanding, and support, pride breeds competition and a desire to elevate oneself above others. This hinders the church's ability to function as a united body, working together for the greater good.

Furthermore, pride inhibits the practice of genuine forgiveness. Prideful individuals often struggle to admit their own faults and seek forgiveness from others. Their inflated sense of self-worth prevents them from acknowledging their mistakes and seeking reconciliation. As a result, bitterness and resentment fester, hindering the transformative power of forgiveness from taking effect. In order to break the chains of resentment, it is imperative for church members to humble themselves and recognize their own need for forgiveness.

Additionally, pride blinds believers to their own limitations and flaws. When pride takes hold, individuals become resistant to correction or guidance, believing that they are always right. This hampers personal growth and spiritual development, as prideful individuals refuse to acknowledge areas in their lives that require improvement. The church is meant to be a place of growth and spiritual maturity, but pride stifles this process, hindering individuals from reaching their full potential.

To combat the dangers of pride, church members must cultivate humility and self-awareness. Recognizing that none of us are without fault and that we all stand in need of forgiveness is essential. Humility opens the door to empathy, understanding, and true fellowship. It encourages individuals to extend grace to one another, fostering an environment of love, unity, and growth.

In conclusion, understanding the dangers of pride is paramount in the pursuit of exploring the transformative power of forgiveness within the church. By recognizing the detrimental effects of pride on unity, forgiveness, and personal growth, church members can actively work towards breaking the chains of resentment. Cultivating humility and self-awareness are key steps towards fostering an environment of love, understanding, and genuine transformation within the church community.

Practical steps to humbling oneself for forgiveness

In the journey towards forgiveness, it is crucial to recognize the importance of humbling oneself. It is through humility that we open our hearts to the transformative power of forgiveness. As church members, we have the unique opportunity to explore this power within the safe and nurturing environment of our faith community. Here are some practical steps to help us humble ourselves and experience the profound healing that forgiveness brings.

1. Reflect on our own shortcomings: To truly humble ourselves, we must first acknowledge our own imperfections and need for forgiveness. Take time to reflect on our actions, attitudes, and words that may have caused harm to others. Recognizing our own faults will help us approach forgiveness with a spirit of compassion and understanding.

2. Seek reconciliation: Humbling ourselves also means being proactive in seeking reconciliation with those we have hurt or have been hurt by. Reach out to the individuals involved and express genuine remorse for our actions. Demonstrate a willingness to listen, understand, and make amends. This step requires courage and vulnerability, but it is an essential part of the forgiveness process.

3. Practice empathy and compassion: Cultivating empathy and compassion towards others is vital in the journey of forgiveness. Put ourselves in the shoes of those who have wronged us, trying to understand their motives and struggles. By doing so, we can develop a greater sense of empathy, which makes it easier to extend forgiveness.

4. Let go of resentment and grudges: Humility requires us to release the burdens of resentment and grudges that we may be carrying. Holding onto these negative emotions only hinders our ability to forgive and move forward. Choose to let go of past grievances, acknowledging that forgiveness is a gift we give ourselves as much as it is for others.

5. Pray for a humble heart: Finally, prayer plays a significant role in humbling ourselves for forgiveness. Seek guidance from a higher power, asking for the strength to let go of pride and embrace humility. Pray for the wisdom to see forgiveness as a transformative process that brings healing and reconciliation.

As church members, we are called to explore the transformative power of forgiveness. By humbling ourselves, practicing empathy, and seeking reconciliation, we can experience the profound healing that forgiveness brings. Let us break the chains of resentment and embrace the liberating power of forgiveness in our lives and within our faith community.

Addressing Misconceptions about Forgiveness

Misconceptions about forgiveness can hinder our ability to experience its transformative power in our lives and within the Church. In this subchapter, we aim to shed light on common misunderstandings surrounding forgiveness and provide a clearer understanding of its true essence.

Firstly, forgiveness is often mistaken for condoning or excusing the wrongdoings of others. However, it is crucial to recognize that forgiveness does not minimize or justify the pain caused by someone's actions. Instead, it involves a conscious decision to release the resentment, anger, and desire for revenge that may be lingering within us. Forgiveness is about freeing ourselves from the chains of resentment, not about absolving the offender of their responsibility.

Another misconception is that forgiveness means forgetting or pretending that the hurtful event never occurred. This belief can be damaging, as it downplays the significance of the pain endured. Forgiveness is not about erasing memories, but rather about letting go of the emotional burden associated with those memories. It is a process of healing and growth, where we acknowledge the pain while choosing to move forward with a renewed sense of peace and wholeness.

Additionally, some may believe that forgiveness requires reconciliation and rebuilding trust with the offender. While reconciliation can be a beautiful outcome of forgiveness, it is not always possible or safe. Forgiveness can occur in the absence of reconciliation, as it primarily involves an inner transformation of the heart. It is a personal journey that allows us to find healing and restore our relationship with God, regardless of the actions of others.

Lastly, forgiveness is sometimes seen as a one-time event, a single act of letting go. However, forgiveness is often a continuous process that may require time, prayer, and support from the church community. It is not always easy, and there may be setbacks along the way. But embracing forgiveness as a way of life can bring about profound personal growth and strengthen the bonds within the Church.

In conclusion, understanding the misconceptions around forgiveness is vital in exploring its transformative power. Forgiveness is not about condoning or forgetting, nor does it always lead to reconciliation. It is an ongoing process that liberates us from the chains of resentment and allows us to experience the true power of forgiveness within ourselves and our church community. By addressing these misconceptions, we can pave the way for a more compassionate, forgiving, and transformative Church.

Debunking myths surrounding forgiveness

When it comes to forgiveness, there are many misconceptions that can hinder our ability to experience its transformative power in our lives. In this subchapter, we will debunk these myths surrounding forgiveness and provide a clear understanding of its significance in our spiritual journey.

Myth 1: Forgiveness means forgetting and condoning the offense.

Contrary to popular belief, forgiveness does not require us to forget or condone the offense committed against us. Forgiveness is a personal choice to let go of the resentment and anger we hold against the offender. It does not mean we excuse their actions or pretend that the hurt never occurred. Instead, forgiveness empowers us to release the burden of bitterness and find healing.

Myth 2: Forgiveness is a one-time event.

Forgiveness is often seen as a single act or event. However, it is a process that unfolds over time. It involves acknowledging our pain, working through our emotions, and gradually releasing the grip of resentment. Forgiveness is a journey that requires patience and self-compassion as we navigate the complexities of our emotions.

Myth 3: Forgiveness is a sign of weakness.

Forgiveness is often misunderstood as a sign of weakness or surrender. In truth, it takes great strength and courage to forgive. It requires us to confront our pain head-on, face our vulnerabilities, and choose compassion over revenge. By forgiving, we break the chains of resentment that hold us captive and discover the power to transform ourselves and our relationships.

Myth 4: Forgiveness means reconciliation.

Another common misconception is that forgiveness automatically leads to reconciliation. While forgiveness can pave the way for reconciliation, it does not guarantee it. Reconciliation requires the willingness and effort of both parties involved. Forgiveness, on the other hand, is a personal decision that liberates us from the pain of the past, regardless of whether or not reconciliation is possible.

Myth 5: Forgiveness is only for the benefit of the offender.

Perhaps the most prevalent myth surrounding forgiveness is that it benefits the offender more than the forgiver. On the contrary, forgiveness is primarily for our own well-being. It allows us to break free from the cycle of resentment and experience true inner peace. By forgiving, we release the negative energy that keeps us trapped and open ourselves up to the transformative power of love and compassion.

In conclusion, it is essential for church members to debunk these myths surrounding forgiveness in order to fully explore its transformative power. By understanding that forgiveness does not mean condoning or forgetting, that it is a process rather than a single act, and that it is a sign of strength rather than weakness, we can embrace the true essence of forgiveness. Let us break the chains of resentment and experience the liberating and healing power of forgiveness in our lives and in our church community.

Clarifying misconceptions about justice and forgiveness

In our journey towards exploring the transformative power of forgiveness, it is crucial to address and clarify some common misconceptions about justice and forgiveness. As church members seeking to break the chains of resentment, we must understand the delicate balance between these two concepts and how they can work together to bring about true healing and reconciliation.

One misconception is that forgiveness means condoning or excusing the wrongdoings of others. This could not be further from the truth. Forgiveness does not mean minimizing or ignoring the gravity of the offense. Instead, it is a conscious choice to let go of the resentment and anger that we hold towards the person who has hurt us. It is acknowledging that the wrongdoing occurred, but refusing to hold onto the negative emotions that keep us trapped in a cycle of bitterness.

Another misconception is that forgiveness negates the need for justice. However, justice is an essential aspect of creating a harmonious society and restoring broken relationships. Forgiveness does not mean that justice should be disregarded or overlooked. Rather, it means that we can pursue justice with a heart that is free from hatred and a desire for revenge. We can advocate for fairness and accountability while still extending grace and mercy towards those who have wronged us.

It is also important to dispel the notion that forgiveness is a one-time event. Forgiveness is a process that often takes time and effort. It may require multiple acts of forgiveness as we continually choose to release the pain and resentment that resurfaces. It is not a sign of weakness to struggle with forgiveness; rather, it is a testament to our humanity and the complexity of our emotions.

Furthermore, forgiveness does not mean that we have to reconcile or trust the person who has hurt us. While forgiveness opens the door to healing, reconciliation is a separate process that involves rebuilding trust and establishing healthy boundaries. It is possible to forgive someone and still maintain distance or even sever ties if necessary for our own well-being.

By clarifying these misconceptions, we can better grasp the true essence of justice and forgiveness. As church members, we have the opportunity to embody these principles and demonstrate to the world the transformative power of forgiveness. It is through forgiveness that we can break free from the chains of resentment and experience deep healing and restoration both individually and within our communities.

Healing Through Empathy and Understanding

In a world marked by hurt, pain, and disappointment, finding healing and peace can seem like an insurmountable task. However, as church members, we have a powerful tool at our disposal - the transformative power of forgiveness. Within the walls of our church, we have the opportunity to break the chains of resentment and embrace a path of healing, empathy, and understanding.

Forgiveness, at its core, is an act of love and compassion. It is not simply an action to be taken, but a mindset to be cultivated. When we choose to forgive, we choose to let go of the anger, bitterness, and grudges that weigh us down. It is in this act of forgiveness that we discover a profound sense of freedom and liberation.

But how do we embark on this journey of forgiveness? It begins with empathy and understanding. We must strive to put ourselves in the shoes of those who have hurt us, seeking to understand the circumstances and motivations behind their actions. This empathetic approach allows us to view the situation from a new perspective, one that fosters compassion rather than resentment.

Through empathy, we can recognize that everyone is flawed and susceptible to making mistakes. We all have our own struggles and wrestle with our own demons. By understanding this universal truth, we can extend grace and forgiveness to others, just as we hope to receive it ourselves.

In the church community, we have a unique opportunity to practice empathy and understanding. We are a diverse group of individuals with different backgrounds, experiences, and perspectives. By embracing this diversity and actively seeking to understand one another, we foster an environment of healing and growth.

Healing through empathy and understanding also requires vulnerability. We must be willing to open our hearts and share our own struggles, allowing others to see our flaws and imperfections. In doing so, we create a safe space where others feel comfortable doing the same. It is through this vulnerability that true healing can take place, as we connect on a deeper level and find solace in our shared humanity.

As church members, let us embrace the transformative power of forgiveness. Let us cultivate empathy and understanding, allowing healing to permeate our hearts and souls. By breaking the chains of resentment, we can create a community that fosters love, compassion, and growth. Together, let us embark on this journey of healing, supporting one another along the way, as we discover the true power of forgiveness in the church.

Cultivating empathy within the church community

In our journey towards spiritual growth and understanding, one of the most powerful tools we have at our disposal is empathy. Empathy is the ability to understand and share the feelings of another person. When we cultivate empathy within our church community, we create an environment where forgiveness and healing can flourish, and where transformative change becomes possible.

Empathy allows us to step into someone else's shoes, to see the world through their eyes, and to truly connect with their pain, struggles, and joys. As church members, it is crucial that we develop and nurture this empathetic mindset, as it enables us to embody the teachings of Jesus Christ and live out his message of love and compassion.

When we cultivate empathy within our church community, we create a safe space for individuals to share their stories, vulnerabilities, and experiences without fear of judgment or rejection. This creates a sense of belonging and fosters a deeper understanding of one another's struggles, which in turn leads to a greater capacity for forgiveness.

Empathy also helps us to break down barriers and overcome divisions within our church community. By actively seeking to understand the perspectives of others, we break free from our own biases and prejudices, allowing for a more inclusive and harmonious environment.

To cultivate empathy within our church community, we can start by practicing active listening. This means giving our full attention to the speaker, without interrupting or passing judgment. It means seeking to understand, rather than simply waiting for our turn to speak.

We can also engage in intentional acts of kindness and compassion, both within our church community and in our daily lives. By actively looking for opportunities to help others and show empathy, we create a ripple effect that extends far beyond our immediate circle.

Additionally, education and awareness are key to cultivating empathy. By learning about various cultures, backgrounds, and experiences, we broaden our perspective and develop a more comprehensive understanding of the human condition.

In conclusion, cultivating empathy within our church community is a powerful way to explore the transformative power of forgiveness. It creates an environment of love, understanding, and acceptance, enabling us to break the chains of resentment and experience true healing. As church members, let us commit to embracing empathy and fostering a community where forgiveness can thrive.

Learning to understand the pain of others

Learning to understand the pain of others is a crucial step in the journey of forgiveness and breaking the chains of resentment. In order to truly embrace the transformative power of forgiveness, church members must develop empathy and compassion towards those who have caused them pain.

Often, when we are hurt by someone, our natural instinct is to focus solely on our own pain and seek justice or revenge. However, as followers of Christ, we are called to a higher standard. We are called to love our enemies and pray for those who persecute us. This requires an understanding of the pain and brokenness that may have led the other person to hurt us.

Understanding the pain of others does not mean excusing or justifying their actions. It means recognizing that hurt people often hurt others. It means acknowledging that the person who caused us pain may have experienced their own trauma, struggles, or feelings of inadequacy. By seeking to understand their pain, we open ourselves up to the possibility of healing and reconciliation.

To truly understand the pain of others, we must be willing to listen and empathize. This requires active and intentional engagement. We cannot simply assume we know what someone else is going through. We must be willing to put ourselves in their shoes, to listen to their stories, and to validate their experiences.

In the church community, it is essential that we create safe spaces for individuals to share their pain and be heard. This can be achieved through support groups, counseling services, or even informal conversations over coffee. By actively seeking to understand the pain of others, we create an environment where healing and forgiveness can flourish.

Learning to understand the pain of others is not an easy task. It requires patience, humility, and a willingness to let go of our own hurt. However, the rewards are immeasurable. As we develop empathy and compassion towards those who have caused us pain, we open ourselves up to the transformative power of forgiveness. We become vessels of healing and agents of reconciliation within our church community.

In conclusion, church members must embrace the subchapter of "Learning to understand the pain of others" as a crucial step in their journey towards breaking the chains of resentment. By actively seeking to understand the pain of others, we create an environment of empathy, compassion, and healing. This subchapter serves as a guide for church members to explore the transformative power of forgiveness and its ability to bring about reconciliation and restoration within the church community.

Chapter 3: The Transformative Journey of Forgiveness

Embracing Vulnerability in the Church

In our journey of faith, we often find ourselves grappling with deep-seated emotions and struggles that hinder our spiritual growth. Resentment, in particular, has the power to chain our hearts and prevent us from experiencing the transformative power of forgiveness. It is within the walls of the church that we seek solace, guidance, and support to break free from these chains and embrace vulnerability.

Embracing vulnerability may seem counterintuitive in a world that often values strength and self-reliance. However, as church members, we must recognize that vulnerability is not a sign of weakness but rather a testament to our trust in God and our willingness to surrender to His plans. It is through vulnerability that we open ourselves up to healing, restoration, and the freedom that forgiveness brings.

When we gather as a church community, it is essential to create an environment where vulnerability is not only accepted but encouraged. We must strive to cultivate a safe space where individuals can share their struggles, doubts, and pain without fear of judgment or rejection. By doing so, we create opportunities for healing and growth, as we realize that we are not alone in our journey but surrounded by fellow believers who have experienced similar challenges.

In embracing vulnerability, we acknowledge that forgiveness is not a one-time event but a continuous process. It requires us to confront our own shortcomings, acknowledge the pain caused by others, and extend grace and compassion. Vulnerability allows us to recognize our need for forgiveness and enables us to extend that same forgiveness to others. It is through vulnerability that we begin to break the chains of resentment and experience the freedom that forgiveness brings.

As church members, we must actively engage in exploring the transformative power of forgiveness. This involves engaging in open and honest conversations, seeking mentorship and guidance from spiritual leaders, and participating in support groups or workshops that focus on forgiveness and healing. By embracing vulnerability, we allow ourselves to fully engage in this transformative process and witness the incredible power of forgiveness in our lives.

In conclusion, embracing vulnerability in the church is crucial for breaking the chains of resentment and experiencing the transformative power of forgiveness. As church members, it is our responsibility to create a safe and nurturing environment where vulnerability is embraced and individuals can find healing, restoration, and freedom. By actively exploring the transformative power of forgiveness, we can unlock the full potential of our faith and live lives that reflect God's love and grace.

Encouraging open communication and transparency

In any community, open communication and transparency are essential for fostering a strong and healthy relationship amongst its members. The same holds true for the church, a place where forgiveness and love should prevail. This subchapter will explore the transformative power of forgiveness in the context of encouraging open communication and transparency within the church community.

Open communication is a fundamental aspect of building trust among church members. When individuals feel safe to express their thoughts, concerns, and even struggles, a supportive and nurturing environment is created. This open dialogue promotes understanding, empathy, and ultimately, forgiveness. By encouraging open communication, the church community can address conflicts and misunderstandings promptly, preventing resentment from taking root and hindering personal and collective growth.

Transparency goes hand in hand with open communication. It involves being honest, genuine, and accountable for one's actions and intentions. When church members practice transparency, they build trust and create an atmosphere of authenticity and vulnerability. This environment allows individuals to share their experiences, seek guidance, and offer support without fear of judgment or rejection. Transparency also helps to dismantle any hidden agendas or secrets that may breed resentment and division within the church.

To promote open communication and transparency, the church leadership can implement various strategies. Regular town hall meetings or forums can be organized to provide a platform for members to voice their opinions and concerns openly. Small group discussions or support circles can be established to facilitate deeper connections and encourage trust-building among individuals. Additionally, workshops or seminars on effective communication and conflict resolution can equip church members with the necessary skills to navigate difficult conversations with grace and humility.

Furthermore, embracing transparency within the church leadership is crucial. Pastors, ministers, and elders should model transparency by openly sharing their own struggles, seeking forgiveness when necessary, and being accountable to the congregation. This vulnerability demonstrates that everyone within the church community is on a journey of growth, and it encourages others to do the same.

In conclusion, encouraging open communication and transparency within the church community is vital for exploring the transformative power of forgiveness. By fostering an environment where individuals can freely express themselves and practicing honesty and accountability, the church becomes a place of healing, growth, and love. Through open communication and transparency, church members can break the chains of resentment and embrace forgiveness, allowing for a more profound connection with one another and with God.

Creating a safe space for vulnerability and healing

In our journey towards exploring the transformative power of forgiveness, it is crucial to create a safe space within our church community where vulnerability and healing can flourish. As church members, we have the unique opportunity to support one another in our pursuit of forgiveness, enabling us to break the chains of resentment and experience true freedom.

First and foremost, it is essential to establish an atmosphere of trust and non-judgment. We must create an environment where individuals feel safe to share their struggles, hurts, and pains without fear of condemnation or gossip. This requires us to cultivate a culture of empathy and compassion, actively listening to others without interrupting or dismissing their experiences.

To foster vulnerability and healing, we must also prioritize confidentiality. When someone opens up about their wounds, it is crucial that we treat their words with utmost respect and discretion. Confidentiality builds trust and encourages others to share their stories, knowing that their privacy will be honored.

In addition, we should encourage open and honest communication. This involves promoting dialogue that is free from defensiveness or personal attacks. By actively listening to one another and speaking with kindness and empathy, we can create an environment that fosters understanding and growth.

Furthermore, creating a safe space for vulnerability and healing requires us to acknowledge and validate the pain experienced by others. We must resist the instinct to minimize or dismiss someone's suffering, recognizing that each person's journey is unique. By acknowledging their pain, we demonstrate our willingness to walk alongside them and offer support in their healing process.

Finally, it is vital to provide resources and opportunities for growth and healing. This can include organizing support groups, workshops, or inviting guest speakers who specialize in forgiveness and healing. By providing these avenues, we empower our church members to seek the help they need and take steps towards their own transformation.

Creating a safe space for vulnerability and healing within our church community is an ongoing journey that requires commitment and intentionality from each member. By fostering trust, confidentiality, open communication, validation, and providing resources, we can support one another in breaking the chains of resentment and embracing the transformative power of forgiveness. Together, we can create a church community that fosters healing, growth, and reconciliation.

The Power of Apology and Reconciliation

In our journey towards spiritual growth, one of the most transformative powers we can explore is that of forgiveness. As church members, we are called to embrace forgiveness not only as a personal practice but also as a means to foster unity and healing within our faith community. However, forgiveness cannot exist in isolation; it requires the power of apology and reconciliation to truly break the chains of resentment.

Apology is an essential first step towards healing and restoration. It takes courage and humility to acknowledge our wrongdoings and take responsibility for the pain we have caused others. As church members, we must recognize that we are not exempt from making mistakes or hurting others. It is through sincere apologies that we demonstrate our commitment to growth, integrity, and love for our fellow brothers and sisters in Christ.

Apology alone, though, is not sufficient. Reconciliation, the act of restoring broken relationships, is the next crucial step. Reconciliation requires deliberate efforts to rebuild trust, to bridge the gaps that resentment has created, and to foster an environment of love, understanding, and acceptance. It is only through reconciliation that we can truly experience the transformative power of forgiveness.

When we extend forgiveness and seek reconciliation, we create space for the Holy Spirit to work within us and our church community. We free ourselves from the burden of holding onto resentment, bitterness, and anger. By embracing the power of apology and reconciliation, we allow God's love to flow through us, healing wounds, restoring brokenness, and uniting us in a bond that is stronger than any offense.

However, it is important to note that forgiveness, apology, and reconciliation are not easy tasks. They require vulnerability, patience, and a deep commitment to personal growth. It may take time, effort, and sometimes even professional help to navigate the complexities of forgiveness and reconciliation. Yet, the rewards are immeasurable.

As church members, let us commit to exploring the transformative power of forgiveness and embracing the vital role of apology and reconciliation in our journey towards spiritual growth. By doing so, we can break the chains of resentment that hinder our personal lives and our church community, fostering an environment of love, healing, and unity that truly reflects the teachings of Christ.

The art of sincere apology

In our journey to explore the transformative power of forgiveness, we must first address the crucial step of offering a sincere apology. As church members, we are called to embody the principles of love, compassion, and forgiveness, both within our community and in our interactions with the world. Yet, we are all fallible beings and sometimes find ourselves in situations where we have hurt or wronged others.

Apologizing sincerely is an art that requires humility, self-reflection, and a genuine desire for reconciliation. It is not merely an act of saying sorry; it is an opportunity to acknowledge our mistakes, take responsibility for our actions, and seek forgiveness with a genuine heart.

The first step in this art is self-reflection. It requires us to honestly examine our own actions and motivations, seeking to understand the impact our behavior has had on others. This self-awareness helps us to recognize the need for an apology and sets the stage for genuine remorse.

When offering an apology, it is important to take ownership of our actions. By admitting our mistakes without making excuses or shifting blame, we demonstrate our sincerity. This requires courage and vulnerability, as we expose our flaws and acknowledge the pain we have caused.

A sincere apology is not complete without expressing remorse and empathy. It is essential to convey genuine sorrow for the hurt we have inflicted and to validate the emotions of those we have wronged. By putting ourselves in their shoes and acknowledging the pain we have caused, we open the door for true healing and reconciliation.

Furthermore, a sincere apology involves making amends. It is not enough to apologize; we must also take concrete steps to rectify the situation and prevent similar harm in the future. This could involve seeking guidance, attending counseling, or implementing changes in our behavior.

Lastly, a sincere apology requires patience and understanding. It is up to the offended party to grant forgiveness, and they may need time to heal and process their emotions. We must be willing to give them the space they need, demonstrating our commitment to their well-being and the restoration of the relationship.

In the transformative power of forgiveness, the art of sincere apology plays a vital role. It allows us to break the chains of resentment that bind us, fostering an environment of love, understanding, and growth within the church community. As we cultivate this art, we become catalysts for healing, reconciliation, and a powerful witness to the world.

Steps towards reconciliation in the church

Introduction:

In a world filled with conflict and division, the church stands as a beacon of hope and unity. However, even within the church, resentment and discord can find their way in, threatening to tear apart the very fabric of the community. It is in these moments that the transformative power of forgiveness becomes crucial. In this subchapter, we will explore the steps towards reconciliation in the church, revealing how forgiveness can mend broken relationships and restore harmony within the body of Christ.

Step 1: Recognize the Need for Reconciliation:

The first step towards reconciliation is acknowledging the existence of brokenness within the church. This requires an honest assessment of our relationships and the willingness to confront the pain and resentment that may have taken root. By recognizing the need for reconciliation, we open the door for healing and restoration.

Step 2: Cultivate a Spirit of Forgiveness:

Forgiveness lies at the heart of reconciliation. It is the decision to release the offender from the debt they owe us, just as Christ forgave us. Cultivating a spirit of forgiveness involves letting go of grudges, bitterness, and the desire for revenge. It is a choice to extend grace and mercy, even when it feels undeserved.

Step 3: Engage in Honest Dialogue:

Reconciliation cannot occur without open and honest communication. It is essential to have courageous conversations with those we have hurt or been hurt by. This requires active listening, empathy, and a willingness to understand the perspective of others. Through dialogue, we can gain clarity, resolve misunderstandings, and find common ground.

Step 4: Seek Mediation and Guidance:

Sometimes, reconciliation may require external assistance. Seeking mediation from a trusted leader or counselor can provide a safe and neutral space for all parties involved. These mediators can help facilitate the healing process, ensuring that everyone's voice is heard and guiding the church towards a resolution that promotes unity.

Step 5: Embrace a Culture of Grace and Restoration:

Reconciliation is an ongoing journey that requires a culture of grace and restoration to thrive. It involves extending forgiveness not only to those who have directly harmed us but also to the entire body of Christ. By embracing a culture of grace, we create an environment where healing is prioritized, and individuals are given the opportunity to grow and change.

Conclusion:

Reconciliation in the church is a powerful testament to the transformative power of forgiveness. By recognizing the need for reconciliation, cultivating a spirit of forgiveness, engaging in honest dialogue, seeking mediation when necessary, and embracing a culture of grace and restoration, we can break the chains of resentment and create a church community that reflects the love and forgiveness of Christ. Through these steps, we can forge stronger relationships, promote unity, and fulfill our calling to be the light of the world.

Cultivating a Culture of Forgiveness

Forgiveness is a powerful tool that has the potential to transform not only individual lives but also entire communities. In our churches, cultivating a culture of forgiveness can have a profound impact on our relationships, our ministries, and our ability to fulfill our mission of spreading God's love.

Exploring the transformative power of forgiveness allows us to break the chains of resentment that often plague our hearts and hinder our spiritual growth. It is only through forgiveness that we can truly experience the freedom and peace that God intended for us. By embracing forgiveness, we release ourselves from the burden of carrying grudges and allow healing to take place in our lives.

As church members, we have a responsibility to create an environment where forgiveness is not only encouraged but also practiced. We must actively seek opportunities to extend forgiveness to one another, understanding that we are all imperfect and in need of God's grace. By modeling forgiveness in our own lives, we inspire others to do the same and create a ripple effect of healing and reconciliation within our church family.

One way to cultivate a culture of forgiveness is through open and honest communication. When conflicts arise, it is crucial that we address them in a spirit of love and humility. Instead of harboring resentment or gossiping, we should strive to resolve conflicts through dialogue and seek reconciliation. This requires active listening, empathy, and a willingness to admit our own faults and seek forgiveness when necessary.

Another important aspect of cultivating a culture of forgiveness is to let go of the past. Holding onto past hurts and grievances only perpetuates a cycle of bitterness and resentment. Instead, we must choose to forgive and let go, allowing God's healing power to work in our hearts. This may require us to surrender our desire for revenge or justice and trust in God's ultimate justice and redemption.

It is also essential to remember that forgiveness does not mean condoning or forgetting the wrong that has been done. Rather, it is a conscious choice to release the offender from the debt we believe they owe us, recognizing our own need for forgiveness from God.

In conclusion, cultivating a culture of forgiveness within our church community is a powerful and transformative act. By exploring the transformative power of forgiveness, we break the chains of resentment and open ourselves up to God's healing and restoration. As church members, we have the responsibility to model forgiveness, practice open communication, and let go of the past. In doing so, we create an environment where forgiveness thrives, enabling us to fulfill our mission of spreading God's love and grace to the world.

Promoting forgiveness as a core value within the church

Introduction:

In our journey of faith, we often face situations that test our ability to forgive. Resentment and grudges can weigh us down, hindering our spiritual growth and straining our relationships. The power of forgiveness, however, has the potential to transform lives and bring healing to our communities. In this subchapter, we will explore the transformative power of forgiveness and how it can be promoted as a core value within the church.

Understanding the Transformative Power of Forgiveness:

Forgiveness is not a sign of weakness but a testament to our spiritual strength. It liberates us from the chains of resentment and allows us to experience inner peace. By forgiving others, we imitate the example of Jesus Christ, who forgave even those who crucified Him. Forgiveness is a transformative act that can mend broken relationships, restore harmony, and inspire growth within our church community.

Creating a Culture of Forgiveness:

Promoting forgiveness as a core value within the church requires intentional effort. We must foster an environment where forgiveness is encouraged, celebrated, and practiced regularly. This can be achieved through sermons, Bible studies, and small group discussions that emphasize the importance of forgiveness in our lives. By sharing testimonies of forgiveness and its positive impact, we can inspire others to embrace this transformative power.

Teaching Forgiveness through Scripture:

The Bible offers numerous teachings on forgiveness that can guide us in our journey towards embracing it as a core value. Scriptures such as Matthew 6:14-15 and Colossians 3:13 remind us of the necessity of forgiving others as we have been forgiven by God. By delving into these passages and exploring their meaning, we can gain a deeper understanding of forgiveness and its significance in our faith.

Practicing Forgiveness in Daily Life:

Promoting forgiveness within the church goes beyond theoretical discussions. It requires us to model forgiveness in our daily lives. This can be done by actively seeking reconciliation, extending grace, and letting go of past hurts. We must create safe spaces within our church community where individuals feel supported in their journey towards forgiveness.

Conclusion:

Promoting forgiveness as a core value within the church is essential for personal and communal transformation. By understanding the transformative power of forgiveness, creating a culture that embraces it, teaching its importance through scripture, and practicing forgiveness in our daily lives, we can break the chains of resentment and experience the true freedom that forgiveness brings. May our church be a beacon of forgiveness, inspiring others to explore this transformative power and fostering unity and love within our community.

Implementing forgiveness practices and rituals

Forgiveness is a transformative power that has the ability to heal wounds, restore relationships, and bring about profound personal growth. In the church, where forgiveness is at the core of our beliefs, it is essential that we actively explore and implement forgiveness practices and rituals. By doing so, we can harness the true power of forgiveness and experience its life-changing effects.

One of the first steps in implementing forgiveness practices is to recognize the importance of forgiveness in our lives. We must understand that holding onto resentment and harboring grudges only hinders our spiritual growth and prevents us from fully experiencing God's love and grace. By embracing forgiveness as a central tenet of our faith, we open ourselves up to a world of possibilities.

A practical way to incorporate forgiveness into our lives is by engaging in regular reflection and self-examination. This can be done through personal prayer or journaling, where we honestly assess our own actions and attitudes towards others. By identifying areas where we may have caused harm or held onto bitterness, we can begin the process of seeking forgiveness both from God and from those we have wronged.

Another powerful forgiveness practice is the act of confession. Within the church community, we can create a safe and supportive environment where individuals can openly acknowledge their mistakes and seek forgiveness from one another. This not only promotes healing and reconciliation but also fosters a sense of humility and vulnerability within the church.

Rituals can also play a significant role in implementing forgiveness practices. For example, the act of taking Communion can serve as a powerful reminder of Christ's ultimate act of forgiveness on the cross. By partaking in this ritual, we are reminded of the importance of extending forgiveness to others as we have been forgiven.

In addition, creating rituals within small groups or prayer circles where individuals can come together to share their forgiveness journeys can be impactful. This creates a sense of community and solidarity, allowing individuals to learn from one another's experiences and offer support as they navigate the complexities of forgiveness.

Implementing forgiveness practices and rituals in the church is a testament to our commitment to living out the teachings of Jesus Christ. By exploring the transformative power of forgiveness, we can break the chains of resentment that hold us back and experience true freedom and restoration. Let us embrace forgiveness as a way of life, both individually and collectively, and witness the incredible power it has to heal and transform our lives.

Chapter 4: Nurturing a Forgiving Heart

Forgiving Ourselves: Letting Go of Guilt and Shame

Subchapter: Forgiving Ourselves: Letting Go of Guilt and Shame

Introduction:

In our journey of exploring the transformative power of forgiveness, it is crucial to address a significant aspect that often lingers in the hearts of many individuals – forgiving ourselves. Guilt and shame have the potential to weigh us down, hindering personal growth and healing. In this subchapter, we will delve into the profound importance of releasing guilt and shame, offering practical steps to embrace self-forgiveness and the freedom it brings.

Understanding Guilt and Shame:

Guilt stems from a sense of wrongdoing, where we carry the burden of our past mistakes and failures. Shame, on the other hand, is a deep-seated belief that we are fundamentally flawed and unworthy of forgiveness or love. These emotions can be particularly potent within a church community, as we hold ourselves to high moral standards.

The Destructive Impact of Guilt and Shame:

Guilt and shame create a toxic environment within our hearts, stifling our spiritual growth and preventing us from experiencing the fullness of God's love and grace. These emotions can lead to self-condemnation, anxiety, and even self-sabotage in our relationships and daily lives.

54

Embracing Self-Forgiveness:

Recognizing that we are all imperfect beings, it is vital to understand that God's love and forgiveness are not limited to others but extend to us as well. By acknowledging our mistakes, seeking forgiveness, and making amends, we open the door to self-forgiveness. It is a conscious choice to let go of guilt and shame, allowing ourselves to heal and grow.

Steps to Self-Forgiveness:

1. Acknowledge and confront our mistakes and shortcomings.

2. Seek forgiveness from God, knowing that His grace is abundant.

3. Practice self-compassion and challenge negative self-talk.

4. Make amends when possible, seeking reconciliation with those we have hurt.

5. Embrace the lessons learned from our past, using them as stepping stones for personal growth.

6. Surround ourselves with a supportive community that encourages and uplifts us.

The Liberating Power of Self-Forgiveness:

As we embark on the journey of self-forgiveness, we find freedom and release from the chains of guilt and shame. Through self-forgiveness, we can fully embrace God's love and grace, allowing it to permeate every aspect of our lives. By extending forgiveness to ourselves, we create space for healing, restoration, and transformation to take place.

Conclusion:

Forgiving ourselves is an essential part of the journey towards breaking the chains of resentment. By recognizing the destructive impact of guilt and shame, we can take intentional steps towards self-forgiveness, embracing the transformative power it holds. As church members, let us cultivate an environment of grace and forgiveness, starting with ourselves, and extending it to others. In doing so, we pave the way for personal growth, healing, and a deeper understanding of the immeasurable love and forgiveness God offers to each one of us.

Understanding the importance of self-forgiveness

In the journey of exploring the transformative power of forgiveness, it is vital for us as church members to understand the significance of self-forgiveness. Oftentimes, we focus on forgiving others who have wronged us, but we often overlook the importance of forgiving ourselves. This subchapter aims to shed light on the profound impact self-forgiveness can have on our lives and our relationship with God.

Self-forgiveness is an act of releasing ourselves from the burden of guilt, shame, and self-condemnation. It involves acknowledging our mistakes, taking responsibility for our actions, and choosing to let go of the negative emotions that may have consumed us. When we embrace self-forgiveness, we open ourselves up to experience healing, restoration, and a renewed sense of self-worth.

One of the key reasons why self-forgiveness is vital is that it allows us to fully receive God's forgiveness. As church members, we understand the importance of seeking God's forgiveness for our sins, but if we fail to forgive ourselves, we may struggle to accept His forgiveness fully. By forgiving ourselves, we align our hearts with God's grace and mercy, allowing Him to work in us and through us more effectively.

Furthermore, self-forgiveness enables us to break free from the chains of resentment that may have bound us for far too long. When we hold onto self-blame and unforgiveness towards ourselves, we hinder our own growth and spiritual transformation. However, by extending forgiveness to ourselves, we open the door for personal growth, self-acceptance, and a deeper understanding of God's unconditional love for us.

Self-forgiveness also empowers us to live a life of freedom and authenticity. When we forgive ourselves, we let go of the past and embrace the present moment with a renewed sense of purpose. We no longer define ourselves by our past mistakes, but rather by the grace and redemption we have received. This enables us to live more authentically, inspiring others with our story of forgiveness and transformation.

In conclusion, self-forgiveness is an essential component of exploring the transformative power of forgiveness in the church. By understanding its importance, we can experience a deeper connection with God, break free from resentment, and live a life of freedom and authenticity. Let us embrace self-forgiveness, allowing it to bring healing, restoration, and a renewed sense of purpose to our lives.

Tools and strategies for self-forgiveness

In our journey towards breaking the chains of resentment and embracing the transformative power of forgiveness, it is important to remember that self-forgiveness is an integral part of the process. As church members, we often find ourselves grappling with guilt, shame, and self-condemnation, hindering our ability to fully experience the freedom and healing that forgiveness offers. This subchapter aims to equip you with practical tools and strategies to cultivate self-forgiveness in your life.

1. Embrace Self-Compassion: Recognize that we are all imperfect beings, prone to making mistakes. Instead of dwelling on our faults, extend the same compassion and understanding to ourselves that we readily offer to others. Remember that God's grace is boundless, and that includes forgiving ourselves.

2. Reflect and Learn: Take time to reflect on the mistakes you have made, acknowledging the impact they may have had on others. Use these experiences as opportunities for growth and self-improvement. Seek guidance from trusted mentors or spiritual leaders who can help you gain perspective and wisdom.

3. Practice Mindfulness: Be present in the moment and observe your thoughts and emotions without judgment. This will enable you to cultivate self-awareness and identify any negative self-talk or self-destructive patterns. Mindfulness also helps you detach from your past actions, allowing space for forgiveness and personal growth.

4. Write a Self-Forgiveness Letter: Put pen to paper and write a heartfelt letter to yourself, expressing remorse for any harm caused and affirming your commitment to change. This exercise can be cathartic and allows you to release any lingering guilt or shame. Revisit this letter whenever you need a reminder of your journey towards self-forgiveness.

5. Seek Accountability: Share your struggles and progress with a trusted friend or mentor within your church community. Accountability partners can offer support, encouragement, and gentle reminders of the importance of self-forgiveness. Together, you can navigate the challenges and celebrate the victories along the way.

Remember, self-forgiveness is not a one-time event but a continuous process. It requires patience, perseverance, and a willingness to extend grace to yourself. As we explore the transformative power of forgiveness within the church, let us not forget the immense power of self-forgiveness. By embracing these tools and strategies, you can break free from the chains of resentment, experience true healing, and live a life filled with love, compassion, and forgiveness.

Extending Forgiveness to Others

In this subchapter, we delve into the profound concept of extending forgiveness to others, exploring the transformative power it holds within the church community. Forgiveness is a fundamental element of our faith, and it is essential for us as church members to understand its true significance and practice it in our lives.

Forgiveness is not an easy task. It requires vulnerability, humility, and a willingness to let go of our resentment and anger. Often, we find ourselves holding onto grudges, allowing bitterness to take root in our hearts. However, by extending forgiveness to others, we can break the chains of resentment and experience true freedom.

One of the key lessons that Jesus taught us was the importance of forgiveness. He not only forgave those who wronged Him but also encouraged us to do the same. As church members, we are called to follow His example and extend forgiveness to those who have hurt us. By doing so, we not only find healing for ourselves but also create an environment of love, grace, and reconciliation within our church community.

Forgiveness is not about condoning the actions of others or sweeping things under the rug. It is a deliberate choice to release the pain and hurt caused by someone else's actions. It is a radical act of love that allows us to move forward, unburdened by the weight of resentment.

When we extend forgiveness to others, we open the door for restoration and reconciliation. It is an opportunity to mend broken relationships and rebuild trust. Forgiveness breaks down walls and fosters unity within the church. It paves the way for healing, both individually and collectively.

However, forgiveness is not a one-time act. It is a continuous process that requires ongoing effort and commitment. Sometimes, we may need to extend forgiveness repeatedly, as old wounds resurface or new offenses occur. But each time we choose forgiveness, we strengthen our faith and deepen our understanding of God's incredible love for us.

In conclusion, extending forgiveness to others is a vital aspect of our Christian journey. It has the power to transform our lives and our church community. By letting go of resentment, we create an environment of love, grace, and reconciliation. Let us embrace the transformative power of forgiveness and break the chains of resentment, allowing God's healing to flow through us and into the world.

Overcoming obstacles in forgiving others

Forgiveness is a fundamental aspect of our faith, yet it can be one of the most challenging tasks we face as church members. In this subchapter, we will explore the obstacles that often hinder our ability to forgive others and discover practical ways to overcome them.

One of the primary obstacles to forgiveness is pride. When someone has wronged us, our egos can prevent us from letting go of the hurt and seeking reconciliation. We may feel justified in holding onto our anger, believing that forgiving would make us appear weak or allow the offender to escape accountability. However, as followers of Christ, we are called to humbly extend forgiveness, just as we have been forgiven by our Heavenly Father.

Another obstacle is the fear of vulnerability. Forgiving someone requires opening ourselves up to the possibility of being hurt again. This fear can make us hesitant to forgive, as we try to protect ourselves from future pain. However, it is important to remember that forgiveness does not mean forgetting or condoning the offense. It is about releasing the burden of resentment and allowing God to heal our hearts.

Unresolved anger can also hinder our ability to forgive. Holding onto anger can feel empowering, as it allows us to maintain a sense of control. However, the longer we hold onto this anger, the more it festers and grows, poisoning our relationships and hindering our spiritual growth. Only by surrendering our anger to God and choosing forgiveness can we experience true freedom and restoration.

Finally, a lack of empathy can prevent us from forgiving others. It is often difficult to put ourselves in the shoes of those who have hurt us, especially when the offense seems unforgivable. However, Jesus calls us to love our enemies and pray for those who persecute us. By seeking to understand the brokenness and pain that may have led someone to hurt us, we can cultivate compassion and find the strength to forgive.

In conclusion, while forgiving others may be challenging, it is a transformative practice that holds immense power in our lives as church members. By overcoming the obstacles of pride, fear, anger, and a lack of empathy, we can experience the true freedom and healing that forgiveness brings. Let us embrace the transformative power of forgiveness and break the chains of resentment in our church community.

Practicing empathy and compassion towards offenders

In our journey of exploring the transformative power of forgiveness, it is essential to discuss the importance of practicing empathy and compassion towards offenders. As church members, we are called to embody the teachings of Christ and extend love even to those who have wronged us. This subchapter aims to shed light on why empathy and compassion are integral to the process of forgiveness and how they can lead to profound healing and reconciliation.

When someone hurts us, it is natural to feel anger, resentment, and the desire for justice. However, holding onto these negative emotions can be detrimental to our own well-being and hinder our spiritual growth. By practicing empathy, we allow ourselves to step into the shoes of the offender and try to understand their perspective. This does not mean condoning their actions, but rather recognizing the complexities of human nature and the multifaceted reasons behind their behavior. By doing so, we open our hearts to the possibility of forgiveness and transformation, both for ourselves and the offender.

Compassion, on the other hand, involves extending kindness and understanding towards others, even when they have caused us pain. It requires us to recognize that offenders, like ourselves, are flawed individuals in need of love and healing. When we approach them with compassion, we create an environment conducive to reconciliation and restoration. Compassion allows us to see beyond the offense and focus on the potential for growth and redemption within each person.

Practicing empathy and compassion towards offenders is not an easy task. It requires patience, humility, and a deep commitment to our faith. However, the rewards are immeasurable. Forgiveness, born out of empathy and compassion, has the power to heal deep wounds, restore relationships, and bring about lasting peace.

As church members, let us strive to be agents of empathy and compassion in a world that often seeks revenge and retribution. Let us remember that forgiveness does not excuse the wrongdoing, but rather frees us from the chains of resentment, allowing us to experience love and joy. By embodying Christ's teachings of empathy and compassion, we can create a community of forgiveness, where healing and transformation become a reality.

In conclusion, practicing empathy and compassion towards offenders is an integral part of our journey towards forgiveness. By understanding the complexities of human nature and extending kindness even to those who have hurt us, we pave the way for healing and restoration. Let us embrace the transformative power of empathy and compassion, and break the chains of resentment that hold us captive.

Sustaining Forgiveness in the Church

In the realm of spirituality, forgiveness holds immense transformative power. It has the ability to heal wounds, mend broken relationships, and bring about personal and communal growth. However, forgiveness is not a one-time act but a continuous journey that requires commitment and effort. For church members seeking to explore and harness the transformative power of forgiveness, it is essential to understand the significance of sustaining forgiveness in the church.

The church, as a community of believers, should be a sanctuary of forgiveness, a place where individuals can find solace, healing, and reconciliation. Sustaining forgiveness within the church is crucial for fostering an environment that allows individuals to experience the transformative power of forgiveness on multiple levels.

Firstly, sustaining forgiveness in the church cultivates an atmosphere of love and acceptance. When church members actively practice forgiveness towards one another, they create a safe space that encourages vulnerability and authenticity. This enables individuals to confront their own resentments and seek forgiveness from others, fostering personal growth and emotional healing.

Secondly, sustaining forgiveness in the church strengthens the bonds of community. Forgiveness is not just an individual act but a communal one. By forgiving one another, church members build trust, unity, and solidarity. As a result, the church becomes a place where relationships are restored, conflicts are resolved, and individuals can experience a sense of belonging and support.

To sustain forgiveness in the church, it is essential to cultivate a culture of empathy and understanding. Church members should be encouraged to practice active listening, seek to understand the perspectives of others, and extend grace and compassion. This enables individuals to empathize with the pain and struggles of others, making forgiveness a more natural and genuine response.

Regular engagement with forgiveness practices and teachings is also crucial for sustaining forgiveness in the church. This can include sermons, small group discussions, workshops, and personal reflection exercises. By consistently exploring the transformative power of forgiveness, church members can deepen their understanding and commitment to forgiveness as a way of life.

Ultimately, sustaining forgiveness in the church is an ongoing process that requires dedication, vulnerability, and intentionality. By actively engaging in forgiveness practices, church members can create a transformative community that embraces love, acceptance, and reconciliation. In doing so, they pave the way for personal and communal healing, growth, and spiritual transformation.

Nurturing forgiveness through ongoing support and accountability

Subchapter: Nurturing Forgiveness through Ongoing Support and Accountability

Introduction:

In our journey towards spiritual growth and transformation, forgiveness plays a crucial role. As church members, we have the unique opportunity to explore the transformative power of forgiveness and cultivate an environment that nurtures healing and reconciliation. In this subchapter, we will delve into the importance of ongoing support and accountability in nurturing forgiveness within our church community.

The Power of Ongoing Support:

Forgiveness is not a one-time event but a continuous process. It requires a supportive community that stands alongside individuals as they navigate the complexities of their emotions and experiences. As church members, we can create a safe space for individuals to share their struggles and receive empathetic understanding. Offering support through prayer, counseling, or simply being present can provide the necessary comfort and encouragement to embark on the path of forgiveness.

Accountability in the Journey of Forgiveness:

Accountability is crucial in fostering a culture of forgiveness within our church. By holding each other accountable, we ensure that forgiveness is not just a theoretical concept but a lived reality. Encouraging open conversations about forgiveness, reminding one another of its importance, and gently challenging any reluctance or resistance can help individuals stay committed to the journey.

Small Groups and Counseling:

Small groups and counseling can be invaluable resources for nurturing forgiveness within our church community. By creating spaces where individuals can share their stories and listen to others, these platforms allow for deeper understanding and empathy. Trained counselors can guide individuals through the process of forgiveness, helping them address underlying wounds and develop strategies for growth.

Education and Resources:

As church members, we must educate ourselves on forgiveness and equip ourselves with the necessary tools to support others. Organizing workshops, inviting guest speakers, or providing resources such as books and articles can empower individuals to explore forgiveness more deeply. By continually expanding our knowledge, we can offer better guidance and support to those seeking to break free from the chains of resentment.

Conclusion:

In our pursuit of spiritual growth, nurturing forgiveness within our church community is of utmost importance. By providing ongoing support and accountability, we create an environment where healing and reconciliation can flourish. Let us commit to exploring the transformative power of forgiveness, not only for our personal journeys but for the greater flourishing of our church and its members. Together, we can break the chains of resentment and embrace the freedom and peace that forgiveness brings.

Fostering a community of grace and understanding

In a world filled with discord and conflict, it is essential for the church to be a beacon of grace and understanding. As church members, we have the unique opportunity to explore the transformative power of forgiveness and create a community that embraces these principles.

Forgiveness is a powerful force that has the ability to break the chains of resentment and free us from the burdens of anger and pain. It is not an easy journey, but one that is essential for personal growth and spiritual well-being. By fostering a community of grace and understanding, we can support each other in this process, creating a safe space for healing and growth.

One of the key aspects of fostering such a community is cultivating empathy. Understanding and acknowledging the pain and struggles of others allows us to extend grace and compassion. By actively listening and seeking to understand, we can create an environment where individuals feel heard and validated. This fosters a sense of belonging and unity, essential for the transformative power of forgiveness to take hold.

Another crucial element is practicing forgiveness ourselves. As church members, we must lead by example, demonstrating the power of forgiveness in our own lives. By openly sharing our own journeys of forgiveness, we can inspire and encourage others to embark on their own paths of healing. Through vulnerability and transparency, we create a space where individuals can feel safe to share their own experiences, doubts, and fears.

Additionally, fostering a community of grace and understanding requires us to confront and address conflict in a healthy manner. Conflict is inevitable, but it is how we handle it that determines the health and unity of our community. By promoting open communication, active listening, and a commitment to reconciliation, we can navigate conflicts in a way that promotes understanding and growth rather than division.

Ultimately, fostering a community of grace and understanding requires intentionality and dedication. It is an ongoing process that requires us to continually examine our own hearts and actions. By actively seeking opportunities to extend grace and understanding, we can create a transformative environment where forgiveness can flourish. As church members, we have the power to break the chains of resentment and create a community that embraces the transformative power of forgiveness.

Chapter 5: The Ripple Effect of Forgiveness in the Church

Healing Broken Relationships

In every community, there are bound to be broken relationships. Whether it's a misunderstanding, a clash of personalities, or a deeply rooted resentment, these fractures can cause significant pain and hinder the growth and harmony of a church. However, there is hope. Through the transformative power of forgiveness, we can mend these broken relationships and create a stronger, more united church community.

Forgiveness is not an easy path to take. It requires courage, humility, and a willingness to let go of our pride and grievances. But when we choose to forgive, we open ourselves up to the possibility of healing and restoration. Instead of holding onto resentment and bitterness, forgiveness allows us to release the chains that bind us, freeing us to experience true peace and joy.

One of the first steps towards healing broken relationships is acknowledging the pain and hurt that has been caused. By recognizing the impact of our actions or the actions of others, we can begin to empathize with each other's struggles and open the door to healing. This process requires open and honest communication, where both parties can express their feelings and perspectives in a safe and non-judgmental environment.

Next, we must cultivate a spirit of empathy and compassion. As church members, we are called to love one another as Christ has loved us. This means extending grace and understanding even when it feels difficult. By genuinely seeking to understand others' experiences and emotions, we create an atmosphere of acceptance and support, which is crucial for the healing process.

Forgiveness also requires us to let go of our desire for revenge or retribution. It's natural to want justice when we have been wronged, but holding onto this desire only perpetuates the cycle of pain and prevents us from moving forward. Instead, we must choose to surrender our grievances to God and trust in His justice. True forgiveness is not about forgetting or condoning the actions that caused the rift but rather releasing our need for vengeance and embracing a spirit of reconciliation.

Finally, healing broken relationships also involves taking practical steps towards reconciliation. This could mean seeking professional help, attending mediation sessions, or engaging in intentional acts of kindness and reconciliation. It requires a commitment to rebuilding trust and investing time and effort into restoring the relationship.

In conclusion, healing broken relationships within our church community is vital for its growth and unity. By exploring the transformative power of forgiveness, we can break the chains of resentment and experience true healing and restoration. Let us embrace forgiveness with open hearts, knowing that through this act, we can build a stronger, more loving church community that reflects the grace and mercy of our Savior.

Restoring harmony within the church community

In the ever-changing landscape of the church, conflicts and resentments are bound to arise. As church members, we are all part of a diverse community with different backgrounds, perspectives, and experiences. It is only natural that disagreements and misunderstandings will occur. However, it is how we handle these conflicts that truly defines the strength of our church community.

This subchapter explores the transformative power of forgiveness and its role in restoring harmony within the church. Forgiveness is not merely a passive act; it is a deliberate choice to release the burden of resentment and seek reconciliation. By exploring the path of forgiveness, we can break the chains that hinder our relationships and embrace a renewed sense of unity.

Firstly, it is important to understand that forgiveness does not mean condoning the actions that caused the resentment. Instead, it allows us to detach ourselves from the negative emotions associated with the conflict. By releasing anger, bitterness, and resentment, we open up space for healing and restoration within our church community.

One of the key aspects of restoring harmony is learning to empathize with others. By putting ourselves in someone else's shoes, we gain insight into their perspective and motivations. This understanding enables us to approach conflicts with compassion and a willingness to seek resolution rather than perpetuate division.

Furthermore, forgiveness requires us to acknowledge our own shortcomings and seek forgiveness from others. By taking responsibility for our actions and humbly seeking reconciliation, we set the stage for healing and unity within the church. This act of vulnerability can foster a culture of forgiveness, where everyone feels safe to admit their mistakes and extend grace to one another.

Restoring harmony within the church community also involves open and honest communication. By actively listening to one another, we can address conflicts before they escalate. This chapter provides practical tools and strategies for effective communication, enabling church members to express their thoughts and emotions in a respectful and constructive manner. Through dialogue, we can foster understanding, resolve conflicts, and strengthen our relationships.

In conclusion, restoring harmony within the church community is a transformative process that requires the power of forgiveness. By embracing forgiveness, empathizing with others, seeking reconciliation, and fostering open communication, we can break the chains of resentment and create a thriving community grounded in love, grace, and unity. Let us embark on this journey together, exploring the transformative power of forgiveness and building a stronger church community.

Rebuilding trust and fostering unity

In a world where resentment and bitterness seem to be pervasive, the church has a unique opportunity to model forgiveness and reconciliation. As church members, we are called to explore the transformative power of forgiveness in order to break the chains of resentment that hold us captive. This subchapter aims to guide us in rebuilding trust and fostering unity within our church community.

Forgiveness is not an easy journey. It requires vulnerability, humility, and a willingness to let go of past hurts. But as we delve into the process of forgiveness, we will discover that it not only liberates the offender but also sets the forgiver free from the burden of anger and resentment. By extending forgiveness, we open ourselves up to the possibility of healing and restoration.

Rebuilding trust is an essential step towards fostering unity within the church. Trust is the foundation upon which strong relationships are built, and without it, divisions and conflicts can arise. It is important for us to acknowledge the pain caused by broken trust and to create safe spaces for honest conversations. Through open dialogue and active listening, we can begin to rebuild trust and bridge the gaps that may have formed.

Unity within the church goes beyond mere agreement on doctrinal matters. It is a deep sense of community and connection that allows us to support and uplift one another. Forgiveness plays a crucial role in fostering this unity. By forgiving one another, we create an environment where grace abounds, and love is demonstrated in tangible ways. This unity becomes a powerful witness to the world, showcasing the transformative power of forgiveness.

As church members, we must actively engage in practices that promote forgiveness and unity. This can include regular prayer for one another, participating in small groups or counseling sessions focused on forgiveness, and seeking reconciliation with those we have hurt or who have hurt us. It is a continuous process that requires intentionality and perseverance.

In conclusion, rebuilding trust and fostering unity within the church is a vital aspect of exploring the transformative power of forgiveness. By embracing forgiveness, we can break the chains of resentment and create a community rooted in love and grace. Let us strive to be a church that embodies forgiveness, healing, and unity, drawing others to experience the transformative power of God's forgiveness in their own lives.

Witnessing the Power of Forgiveness

In the journey of exploring the transformative power of forgiveness, one cannot overlook the profound impact it has within the church community. As church members, we are called to be ambassadors of love, compassion, and forgiveness. However, we often find ourselves struggling with unresolved resentments and grudges that hinder our spiritual growth and harmony within the body of Christ.

This subchapter delves into the firsthand experiences of individuals who have witnessed the remarkable power of forgiveness in their lives and within their church family. It serves as a testament to the incredible healing and restoration that forgiveness can bring, not only to individuals but also to the collective faith community.

Forgiveness has the power to break the chains of resentment that bind us, freeing us to experience true peace and reconciliation. It is through forgiveness that we can release the burden of anger, bitterness, and hurt, allowing God's love to flow through us and transform our relationships.

Within the church, forgiveness has the potential to mend broken relationships, restore trust, and create a safe and nurturing environment for spiritual growth. Through genuine forgiveness, we can dismantle the walls of division and create a united front, enabling us to fulfill our purpose as the body of Christ.

The stories shared in this subchapter highlight the miraculous power of forgiveness. We will hear testimonies of individuals who have forgiven those who have wronged them, leading to personal healing, restored relationships, and even reconciliation with estranged family members. These stories will serve as powerful reminders of the transformative power forgiveness holds and how it can shape our lives and our faith community.

Witnessing the power of forgiveness firsthand can inspire and encourage church members to embark on their own journey of forgiveness. It provides a roadmap for those struggling with resentment, offering practical steps and biblical guidance to break free from the chains of bitterness.

Ultimately, this subchapter aims to ignite a collective desire within the church to embrace forgiveness as a core value, to extend grace and mercy to one another, and to experience the redemptive power of forgiveness. It emphasizes the importance of forgiveness in fostering a thriving and unified church community, and how it can bring us closer to God's heart and His perfect plan for our lives.

Sharing personal stories of forgiveness and transformation

In this subchapter, we will delve into the power of personal stories of forgiveness and transformation within the context of the church. Forgiveness is a central theme in Christianity, and it is through forgiveness that we can experience profound transformation. By exploring the personal stories of individuals who have embarked on this journey, we can gain insight into the transformative power of forgiveness and how it can impact our own lives.

One such story is that of Sarah, a church member who struggled with deep resentment towards her estranged father. For years, Sarah carried the burden of bitterness and anger, feeling trapped in her own emotional prison. However, through her faith and the guidance of her church community, Sarah found the strength to forgive her father. This act of forgiveness not only freed her from the chains of resentment but also allowed her to rebuild a relationship with her father based on love and understanding. Sarah's story serves as a powerful reminder that forgiveness has the ability to mend broken relationships and bring healing to our lives.

Another inspiring story comes from Mark, who experienced a life-altering transformation through forgiveness. Mark had made numerous mistakes in his past, leading him to feel unworthy of God's love and forgiveness. However, through the support and encouragement of his church family, Mark was able to embrace the transformative power of forgiveness and find redemption in his life. By forgiving himself and seeking forgiveness from those he had harmed, Mark experienced a profound spiritual renewal and discovered a new purpose in serving others.

These personal stories highlight the transformative power of forgiveness within the church community. As church members, we must recognize the importance of sharing our personal stories of forgiveness and transformation. By doing so, we can inspire others and create a supportive environment where individuals can find the strength to embark on their own journeys of forgiveness.

Through these stories, we can explore the various aspects of forgiveness, such as letting go of grudges, seeking reconciliation, and experiencing spiritual growth. Additionally, these narratives can provide practical guidance on how to navigate the complexities of forgiveness, offering hope and encouragement to those who may be struggling with resentment.

Ultimately, sharing personal stories of forgiveness and transformation within the church not only strengthens our faith community but also helps us to explore the transformative power of forgiveness in our own lives. By embracing forgiveness, we can break the chains of resentment and experience true freedom, healing, and spiritual growth.

Inspiring others to embrace forgiveness in their lives

Subchapter: Inspiring Others to Embrace Forgiveness in Their Lives

Introduction:

In this subchapter, we will explore the transformative power of forgiveness and how it can positively impact our lives as church members. Forgiveness is not only a personal journey but also a communal one. As believers, it is our responsibility to inspire and encourage others to embrace forgiveness in their lives. By doing so, we can break the chains of resentment and pave the way for healing and reconciliation within our church family.

Understanding the Transformative Power of Forgiveness:

Forgiveness is a powerful force that can liberate us from the burden of anger, bitterness, and resentment. It is a decision to let go of the hurt caused by others and to release ourselves from the emotional bondage that holds us back. When we choose to forgive, we open ourselves up to receiving God's grace and experiencing true inner peace.

Leading by Example:

As church members, it is essential for us to lead by example and demonstrate the transformative power of forgiveness in our own lives. By sharing our personal stories of forgiveness and the healing it brought, we can inspire others to embark on their own journey towards forgiveness. When others witness the positive changes in our lives, they become more open to embracing forgiveness themselves.

Creating a Culture of Forgiveness:

To inspire others to embrace forgiveness, we must strive to create a culture of forgiveness within our church community. This can be done through sermons, Bible studies, and small group discussions that focus on forgiveness and its significance in our Christian walk. By providing resources, support, and a safe space for individuals to share their struggles, we can foster an environment where forgiveness is encouraged and celebrated.

Extending Forgiveness Beyond the Church:

Forgiveness is not limited to our church community; it extends to our interactions with the world around us. As church members, we have the opportunity to demonstrate forgiveness in our workplaces, schools, and neighborhoods. By practicing forgiveness in these areas, we can be a witness to others and inspire them to embrace forgiveness in their own lives.

Conclusion:

As church members, we have a unique opportunity to explore and embrace the transformative power of forgiveness. By leading by example, creating a culture of forgiveness, and extending forgiveness beyond the church, we can inspire others to let go of resentment and experience the freedom that forgiveness brings. Let us break the chains of resentment and embrace forgiveness as a way of life, both individually and collectively, within our church community.

Spreading Forgiveness Beyond the Church

In the book "Breaking the Chains of Resentment: The Power of Forgiveness in the Church," we have explored the transformative power of forgiveness within the church. However, forgiveness is not limited to the walls of our congregations; it has the potential to spread far beyond our immediate community and impact the world around us. In this subchapter, we will delve into the importance of spreading forgiveness beyond the church and the profound effect it can have on individuals and society.

As church members, we are called to be ambassadors of Christ's love and forgiveness. This means extending forgiveness not only to our fellow believers but also to those outside our faith. By embodying forgiveness in our interactions with others, we can inspire and encourage them to embrace this transformative power in their own lives.

In a world plagued by division, conflict, and resentment, the act of forgiveness can be a powerful agent of change. When we choose to forgive, we break the chains of resentment that bind us, and in doing so, we create space for healing and reconciliation. By spreading forgiveness beyond the church, we can contribute to building a more harmonious and compassionate society.

One way to spread forgiveness is through acts of service and kindness. By reaching out to those who have wronged us or holding no grudges against them, we demonstrate the power of forgiveness in action. These acts can inspire others to reflect on their own capacity for forgiveness and consider embracing it in their own lives.

Moreover, our forgiveness should not be limited to personal interactions but should extend to societal issues as well. We can actively engage in initiatives that promote justice, compassion, and reconciliation, advocating for forgiveness as a means to address conflicts and heal wounds. By advocating for forgiveness beyond the church, we can contribute to the transformation of our communities and the world at large.

It is important for church members to remember that forgiveness is not a one-time event but a lifelong journey. As we continue to explore the transformative power of forgiveness in our own lives, let us also strive to spread this message to others. By sharing our stories, experiences, and insights, we can inspire others to embark on their own journey towards forgiveness, ultimately creating a ripple effect that reaches far beyond the confines of our church walls.

In conclusion, spreading forgiveness beyond the church is an essential part of our mission as church members. By embodying forgiveness in our interactions, engaging in acts of service and advocacy, and sharing our experiences with others, we can contribute to building a more forgiving and compassionate world. Let us be bold and courageous in spreading the transformative power of forgiveness, for it has the potential to heal wounds, mend relationships, and bring about lasting change.

Extending forgiveness to the wider community

In our journey of exploring the transformative power of forgiveness, it is essential that we not only focus on healing ourselves but also extend forgiveness to the wider community. As church members, we are called to be instruments of love, compassion, and forgiveness in our interactions with others. By doing so, we can break the chains of resentment and foster reconciliation, not just within our church walls, but also in the broader society.

Extending forgiveness to the wider community begins with acknowledging that we are all interconnected. Our actions, whether positive or negative, have ripple effects that reach far beyond our immediate circle. Therefore, by embracing forgiveness, we can contribute to a collective healing process that has the potential to transform lives and communities.

One way to extend forgiveness is by actively engaging in acts of reconciliation. This involves reaching out to those who have wronged us or have been wronged by others and seeking to restore broken relationships. It requires a willingness to listen, understand, and empathize with those who have caused pain or have been hurt. Through open dialogue and genuine forgiveness, we can bridge the gaps that divide us and build a stronger, more harmonious community.

Another powerful way to extend forgiveness is through acts of service and compassion. By showing kindness and understanding to those who may have been marginalized or excluded, we embody the true essence of forgiveness. This includes embracing the outcasts, offering a helping hand to those in need, and promoting social justice within our community. Through these actions, we create an environment where forgiveness becomes a lived reality, and the transformative power of forgiveness can be experienced by all.

It is important to note that extending forgiveness to the wider community does not mean condoning or overlooking wrongdoing. Rather, it is a conscious choice to let go of resentment, anger, and bitterness, and instead, cultivate a spirit of love and reconciliation. It is about recognizing the inherent worth and dignity of every individual, regardless of their past actions, and offering them an opportunity for redemption and transformation.

As church members, we have a unique opportunity and responsibility to be ambassadors of forgiveness in the wider community. By embodying the principles of forgiveness and extending it to all, we can contribute to a world that is more compassionate, just, and united. Let us break the chains of resentment that hold us back and embrace the power of forgiveness, not only within our church but also in the broader society, for the betterment of all.

Becoming agents of change in a broken world

In a world filled with brokenness, pain, and resentment, it is crucial for us, as church members, to embrace our role as agents of change. We have been called to be beacons of light, spreading hope, love, and forgiveness in a society that is often devoid of these virtues. This subchapter aims to explore the transformative power of forgiveness and how it can empower us to become agents of change in our broken world.

Forgiveness is a concept deeply rooted in the teachings of Jesus Christ. As church members, we are encouraged to follow His example and extend forgiveness to others. However, forgiveness is often misunderstood as a sign of weakness or a way to condone wrongdoing. On the contrary, forgiveness is a powerful tool that can break the chains of resentment and bring about healing and restoration.

When we choose to forgive, we release the burden of anger, bitterness, and revenge that often weigh us down. By letting go of these negative emotions, we open ourselves up to the transformative power of God's love and grace. In doing so, we not only experience personal healing but also become vessels through which God's love can flow to others.

As agents of change, we must first recognize the brokenness around us. It may be evident in our communities, families, or even within the church itself. By acknowledging this brokenness, we can begin to actively seek ways to bring about positive change. This can range from offering a listening ear to someone in pain, to initiating conversations about forgiveness and reconciliation within our church community.

Furthermore, as we explore the transformative power of forgiveness, we must also examine ourselves and our own need for forgiveness. None of us are perfect, and we all make mistakes. It is essential for us to humble ourselves and seek forgiveness when we have wronged others. By doing so, we not only model the behavior we hope to see in others but also create an environment of grace and mercy within the church.

In conclusion, becoming agents of change in a broken world requires us to tap into the transformative power of forgiveness. By extending forgiveness to others, we break the chains of resentment and create opportunities for healing and restoration. As we embrace this concept, we become beacons of light, spreading hope, love, and forgiveness in a world that desperately needs it. Let us, as church members, embrace our role as agents of change and work towards a more forgiving and compassionate society.

Conclusion: Embracing the Freedom of Forgiveness in the Church

As we come to the end of this transformative journey, we find ourselves standing at the threshold of a new chapter in our lives as church members. We have explored the power of forgiveness, delving into the depths of its healing and transformative abilities. Now, it is time to embrace the freedom that forgiveness brings and allow it to permeate every aspect of our lives within the church community.

Forgiveness is not an easy path to tread. It requires us to confront our deepest wounds and face the pain that has held us captive for far too long. But as we have discovered throughout this book, forgiveness is the key that unlocks the chains of resentment and sets us free. It is a gift that we can offer to others and to ourselves, a gift that not only brings healing but also paves the way for reconciliation and restoration within the church.

In embracing the freedom of forgiveness, we must first acknowledge that forgiveness does not mean forgetting or excusing the wrongdoing. It does not negate the need for justice or accountability. Instead, forgiveness is a choice to release the grip of anger, bitterness, and resentment that has bound us. It is a choice to extend grace and mercy, just as God has extended it to us.

By embracing forgiveness, we create an atmosphere of love, compassion, and understanding within the church community. We become a living example of the transformative power of forgiveness, inspiring others to embark on their own journey towards healing. As church members, we have a responsibility to cultivate an environment where forgiveness is not only encouraged but also practiced.

Let us be a community that listens without judgment, offers support without conditions, and extends forgiveness without hesitation. Let us be a community that acknowledges our own faults and shortcomings, recognizing that we too are in need of forgiveness. In doing so, we create a safe space for individuals to heal, grow, and thrive in their relationship with God and with one another.

As we conclude this book, let us remember that forgiveness is not a one-time act but a lifelong journey. It is a choice that we must make daily, as we encounter new hurts and wounds. Let us continually seek God's guidance and strength to embrace the freedom of forgiveness, knowing that through it, we can truly break the chains of resentment and experience the fullness of God's love and grace within the church.

May the transformative power of forgiveness continue to shape and mold us, as we strive to be a community that reflects the heart of Christ, extending forgiveness and healing to all who enter our doors.

End of Subchapter